CAMELS

by JoAnn Early Macken

Reading consultant: Susan Nations, M.Ed., author/literacy coach/consultant

WEEKLY WR READER®
EARLY LEARNING LIBRARY

Please visit our web site at: **www.earlyliteracy.cc**
**For a free color catalog describing Weekly Reader® Early Learning Library's
list of high-quality books, call 1-877-445-5824 (USA) or 1-800-387-3178 (Canada).
Weekly Reader® Early Learning Library's fax: (414) 336-0164.**

Library of Congress Cataloging-in-Publication Data

Macken, JoAnn Early, 1953-
    Camels / by JoAnn Early Macken.
      p. cm. — (Animals I see at the zoo)
    Summary: Photographs and simple text introduce the physical characteristics
and behavior of camels, one of many animals kept in zoos.
    Includes bibliographical references and index.
    ISBN 0-8368-3267-1 (lib. bdg.)
    ISBN 0-8368-3280-9 (softcover)
    1. Camels—Juvenile literature. [1. Camels. 2. Zoo animals.] I. Title.
QL737.U54M34   2002
599.63'62—dc21   2002016889

This edition first published in 2002 by
Weekly Reader® Early Learning Library
330 West Olive Street, Suite 100
Milwaukee, WI 53212 USA

Art direction: Tammy Gruenewald
Production: Susan Ashley
Photo research: Diane Laska-Swanke
Graphic design: Katherine A. Goedheer

Photo credits: Cover, pp. 11, 15 © William Muñoz; title, pp. 9, 19, 21 © James P. Rowan; p. 5
© Ken Lucas/Visuals Unlimited; p. 7 © Rudolph Arndt/Visuals Unlimited; p. 13 © Science VU/Visuals
Unlimited; p. 17 © Bob Newman/Visuals Unlimited

Printed in the United States of America

1 2 3 4 5 6 7 8 9 06 05 04 03 02

Note to Educators and Parents

Reading is such an exciting adventure for young children! They are beginning to integrate their oral language skills with written language. To encourage children along the path to early literacy, books must be colorful, engaging, and interesting; they should invite the young reader to explore both the print and the pictures.

Animals I See at the Zoo is a new series designed to help children read about twelve fascinating animals. In each book, young readers will learn interesting facts about the featured animal.

Each book is specially designed to support the young reader in the reading process. The familiar topics are appealing to young children and invite them to read — and re-read — again and again. The full-color photographs and enhanced text further support the student during the reading process.

In addition to serving as wonderful picture books in schools, libraries, homes, and other places where children learn to love reading, these books are specifically intended to be read within an instructional guided reading group. This small group setting allows beginning readers to work with a fluent adult model as they make meaning from the text. After children develop fluency with the text and content, the book can be read independently. Children and adults alike will find these books supportive, engaging, and fun!

— Susan Nations, M.Ed., author, literacy coach, and consultant in literacy development

I like to go to the zoo. I see camels at the zoo.

Camels come from the **desert**, where it is dry. They can go for days with no water.

Camels have **humps** on their backs. Each hump is a lump of fat.

humps

Some camels have one hump. Some camels have two humps.

Camels can
live on the fat
in their humps.

Camels can walk for days. When a camel walks, its head bobs up and down. Its body sways from side to side.

Camels eat as they walk. They eat plants, twigs, and even sharp thorns.

In the zoo, camels eat hay.

I like to see
camels at the
zoo. Do you?

Glossary

desert — dry land with few plants

hay — grass or other plants cut and dried for animal food

humps — rounded lumps of fat on camels' backs

For More Information

Books

Arnold, Carolyn. *Camel*. New York: Morrow Junior
Books, 1992.

Burnie, David. *Mammals. Eyewitness Explorers* (series).
New York: Dorling Kindersley, 1998.

Web Sites

Canadian Museum of Nature

www.nature.ca/notebooks/english/camel.html

For camel facts and a camel illustration

Lincoln Park Zoo

zoo.interaccess.com/tour/factsheets/mammals/
bactrian_camel.html

For a camel photo and facts

Chaffee Zoo

www.chaffeezoo.org/zoo/animals/camel.html

For a camel photo and facts

Index

About the Author

JoAnn Early Macken is the author of a rhyming picture book, *Cats on Judy*, and *Animal Worlds*, a series of nonfiction picture books about animals and their habitats. Her poems have been published or accepted by *Ladybug*, *Spider*, *Highlights for Children*, and an anthology, *Stories from Where We Live: The Great Lakes*. A winner of the Barbara Juster Esbensen 2000 Poetry Teaching Award, she teaches poetry writing. She lives in Wisconsin with her husband and their two sons.